FINANCIAL FREEDOM

FINANCIAL FREEDOM

Building Wealth and Security for a Brighter Future

ROWAN EVERHART

QuantumQuill Press

CONTENTS

CHAPTER 1

Introduction

Living through our retirement years in comfort and with peace of mind will require some serious dedication. Preparation is the key. By making smart decisions and planning for the future now, we can achieve a level of financial freedom that will provide for a comfortable and satisfying lifestyle throughout our retirement years. Financial freedom is having the knowledge, ability, and freedom to make sound financial choices that best serve our life goals. A young person in debt with student loans, an old person facing costly medical bills; neither has freedom, for they have financial burdens that prevent them from living life as they choose. This book will show you how to attain financial freedom, security, and peace of mind through the building of wealth and the safeguarding of assets.

Parallel to the increase in non-traditional employment, the concept of retirement is getting a makeover as well. The government system is strained and will not be able to sustain itself throughout our lifetimes. The burden of retirement will fall completely on us, and it will be our own responsibility to see that we close our careers in comfort. The age at which a person can realistically retire is getting older and older, and studies have shown that many people simply never do, working into their seventies and eighties out of necessity. In a world that promises longer life expectancy, this is not the best solution. The golden years of life should be spent doing just that, living.

We live in a world of abundant opportunity, but along with it comes a great deal of uncertainty. Change is happening faster than we can keep up with, and where our parents had security with the concept of a job for life, many of us have a hard time holding one down. More and more people are stepping out on their own, choosing unconventional career paths and forgoing employment altogether, putting the responsibility of their financial future squarely on their own shoulders.

CHAPTER 2

Understanding Financial Freedom

In short, financial freedom is the power to be able to make choices.

Financial freedom is also the point at which you have achieved financial security, or the ability to weather a financial storm. This gives peace of mind in knowing that if any negative life event should come to pass, be it illness, loss of job, or some other income reduction, you are able to get through it without it affecting your long-term financial situation.

Financial freedom provides greater opportunities to give back to society and help others. People who are financially free can make choices to work on things that are important, but are not financially rewarding. This can be anything from volunteer work, to a hobby, or a passion to start a business. Many people never have the opportunity to work on something they truly enjoy because they need to keep working at a job they dislike in order to pay the bills.

Financial freedom can mean different things to different people. At its most basic level, financial freedom is the ability to no longer depend on income from employment. This is not to say that all people seek to stop working because they have reached a point of financial freedom. Many people prefer to continue to work because they enjoy what they do. It is about having options to do different things with one's life instead of being forced to do something because of financial necessity.

CHAPTER 3

Setting Financial Goals

Goals provide direction for your financial plans. There are three basic rules for developing goals: write them down, be specific, and give them a deadline. The first part consists of thinking of a permanent goal that is your deepest desire. Accomplishing this fundamental goal should bring you and your loved ones long-term benefit, true happiness, and develop quality of life. Permanent goals can be having a comfortable retirement, sending your children to college, a particular vocation, or forming your own business. Next, determine which steps you would take within the next five years to satisfy your permanent goal. These are your intermediate-term goals that are steps to satisfy the permanent goal. They should not be too specific but are as important because they will provide the means for the next set of goals and lay the foundation for investment choices. The second part of setting financial goals is to determine your current and expected net worth. Net worth is the difference between what you own and the source of financial resources. Calculate your expected net worth at the time when your next set of goals can be met. With the information of where you are now, where you want to be, and the time frame to get there, you can now develop a plan to attain your goals. This is the final part which involves asset accumulation and the risk management which will be discussed throughout the next set of modules.

CHAPTER 4

Creating a Budget

It can be difficult to know how much you may spend on things such as food or your various bills. It is a good idea to keep track of your spending for a month to see exactly where your money goes. This will also give you an idea of where you can make some changes to enhance your financial situation. Once you have done this, setting a limit on various expenses will prevent money from being wasted, ensure you pay your bills on time, and have money left over. This, in turn, will enhance peace of mind.

A budget is a personal spending plan that helps an individual allocate future income. Creating a realistic budget is an effective way to manage your financial situation. It is not hard to do and it means you are in control. It also allows you to make changes where necessary to ensure you avoid any financial difficulties.

CHAPTER 5

Saving and Investing

An article on personal finance would never be complete if it did not discuss the ways one should manage his/her income. It does not matter if the person is earning a little amount of money or a big amount, it is still imperative to manage it the best way possible. This also applies to people who are still earning money for a living, like fresh graduates and part-time workers. It is a common misconception for people that are still in the low level of income that it is still early for them to save. The truth is there is no better time to save than now; also saving money while still having a low income can help kick-start a habit that can help a person prosper financially in the future. This principle is also applicable for people who think that they are earning an adequate amount of money. Oftentimes these people spend all their income without knowing exactly where their money went. Managing income is the first step to financial management and wealth building. This involves detailed planning on where the next income should go and understanding where the last income went. With a well-formulated income management plan, a person can evaluate his current financial position and take the necessary steps.

CHAPTER 6

Managing Debt

If you have debt, you are not alone. Debt is a pervasive problem in our culture. We are a society based on consumerism. In the last 50 years, we have moved from a society that believed in saving and buying to one that believes in borrowing and buying. Easy credit has allowed us to consume more than we earn. The average U.S. household has more than $9,000 in credit card debt. It is as important to learn how to restructure and manage existing debt as it is to avoid future debt problems. Don't be fooled into thinking that you need to pay a debt management company to help you get out of debt. It's not hard to do, you can do it yourself, and the potential savings are significant. You should be wary of consumer credit counseling agencies. Many are reputable organizations that are truly there to help, but others are no more than for-profit debt consolidators that may do more harm than good for your credit and your peace of mind. To reassess your debt, contact the National Foundation for Consumer Credit (800-388-2227), to find a certified consumer credit counselor. A financial planner can help you, as well. Look for the professional designation of Certified Financial Planner (CFP). Many CFPs have experience in helping consumers get out of debt.

CHAPTER 7

Building an Emergency Fund

A personal disaster is bad enough, but adding financial problems into the equation just makes things worse.

The amount of an emergency fund is also dependent on the household income, the stability of this income, and also if the household has any dependents. If you have a relatively secure job with few dependents, then perhaps three months' income may be sufficient. This amount should be established on the basis of whether a job loss or other income reduction would affect the funders. If so, a larger safety net is required for peace of mind.

Set a realistic goal that you feel is within reach. Whether this is a certain percentage of income put aside each month, a nominal amount weekly or monthly, or the capture of windfalls such as bonuses, tax refunds, gifts, and so on.

In the event of any unforeseen crisis, you must then resort to either incurring debt through credit cards and loans, or in some extreme cases, cashing in long-term savings plans, eroding the future financial security. This can all be avoided, no matter how low your income. So, do not be tempted to borrow money to get started. Avoid credit and loans at all costs.

An emergency fund is your safety net for the unexpected. It is there to be used in the event of an unforeseen misfortune. However, the inability to cope financially when disaster strikes is a common problem due to the lack of any safety net.

CHAPTER 8

Protecting Your Assets

I'm not saying this to scare you. The world is not an overly danger-ous place, and most people will live their lives without the vast majority of such problems or knowing anyone who has experienced them. How-ever, it is wise to give thought as to how you can protect yourself against such threats to your assets, how you can ensure that they will be deployed according to your wishes, and how you can provide for a safety net to rebuild should something go wrong.

In this day and age, protecting those assets is vital. It's unrealistic to expect that any individual will be able to relax and watch his/her assets continue to grow without enjoying some high quality of life. Whether the goal is to travel around the world or ensure a successful future for your children, chances are you will need to convert some portion of your assets into income. Unfortunately, there are countless things that can go wrong on this journey. Lawsuits, accidents, premature death, long-term illness, natural disasters, and inappropriate investment in a tax shelter are just a few examples of threats that can decimate your hard-earned assets.

You spend a lifetime accumulating assets. Many people build a comfortable nest egg for themselves and their heirs. These assets include everything from the obvious (house, car, stocks, etc.) to the less tangible (retirement funds, life insurance, etc.).

CHAPTER 9

Building Passive Income Streams

Step three, it is now time to build your passive income. This can be done with several investment opportunities, and each has its own degree of risk. Before you decide what to invest in, take the time to learn about each investment and always consider the risk involved. An option for a lower risk investment could be Ontario Savings Bonds. This guarantees your original investment and there is a guaranteed interest every year. A higher risk investment with the potential for a higher return could be in stocks or mutual funds. This is where you're buying ownership in a company with the hope of the company doing well and the stock price increasing. If the company is successful, so are you. Always try to invest a little at a time and do not place all of your money in one thing.

Step two, you will then need to assess your financial situation. This can be done by sitting down with a financial planner to see what options are available for you. They can also help to set clear and crucial goals. Goals are very important; they give you something to work towards the achievement. An example of a goal could be to generate $20,000 a year in passive income.

To begin the process of building your passive income, you must first start by recognizing how important it is to save your money. How did you know you're paid to income when at the end of the month you have no extra money to show for it? My friend, this is not a good thing. What you should do is to be able to have some money left over after paying all of your bills. This money will then be saved to start your passive income journey.

CHAPTER 10

Real Estate Investment

If you are in a higher income bracket with your regular job or other business, it may be a good idea to take out a loan that will incur deductible interest to invest in a property or something else with a higher rate of return. The money that is borrowed will have a relatively low cost because of the tax deduction on the interest. This is similar to the previous paragraph in the sense that you will be trying to increase your rate of return on an investment of money with a low borrowing cost.

Another way to take advantage of leverage is to only pay the interest on a loan in which the principal would be due in full at the end of the loan. If money is borrowed and then invested into something that will provide a rate of return higher than the rate at which the money was borrowed, it is a profitable investment. This given principle can be hard to achieve and can prove to be very risky, it should be tested on a small scale at first to have a better understanding of it.

Real estate is one of the easiest ways to gain leverage, the use of borrowed money to increase the potential return of an investment. If done prudently, leverage can amplify potential return. A 20% down payment on a mortgage, for example, gets you 100% of the house you want to buy (leverage), assuming the value of the house does not go down. A positive return on investment would be the money earned from rent less the mortgage payment and other losses. Say you bought a $100,000 house and you put $20,000 down, that is what the house is worth now. If you can rent out the house monthly for $750 and the mortgage payment is $650, you are earning a return on the $20,000 cash down payment. If you can rent the house out for $750 a month and your monthly expenses, including mortgage, are $650, you will earn $100 a month in profit or $1,200 annually. This is a 6% return on a $20,000 investment, cash flow on cash. If you factor in the appreciation of the home and market value of the home to increase over time, this may be a 10% annual return on investment.

Leverage

Real estate has become a common investment vehicle and it continues to be popular despite a very rocky market correction in 2007-2010. With low interest rates, many believe it is a great time to buy. Real estate investing offers many ways to make money compared to other investments, one such way is the use of leverage.

CHAPTER 11

Stock Market Investing

The stock market is a big gamble and you could lose a lot of money. If you are new to investing, then it is wise to begin with conservative stocks or even a mutual fund. As you become more experienced, you can play the market more. Conservative stocks are a low risk compared to their potential reward. In basic terms, this means that you will most likely get a little return on a short period investment. With stocks, the longer you invest your money, the higher the chance of higher return. On the same hand, the longer you invest, the higher chance of you losing money. Considerably, it's a low risk, high reward offer. Step 1 would tie in to step 2 very well. Starting off with a small investment for an infrequent return with a method to high return with a low investment. Step 3 on playing the market is physically the game of high risk high return though. This involves a lot of research on your part. You will want to learn the stocks and what effects their changes. Often times if you are all for the high reward, you'll want to invest in small companies because an increase of even $1 in their stock can mean a much higher percentage return. People who do invest in stock will make a lot more than other jobs compared to the time spent researching. This is essentially a typical investment to any other, but research is the key factor. If you tried this during a global recession period, you could lose massive amounts of money! High risk high reward is essentially put on bigger companies. The market for high risk stock is usually at times of large uncertainty in the market, often before a recession or before an increase in the economy. You would have to research which companies have had large change and what they have done to cause such change. An example of recent high uncertainty stock is the BP oil spill. Their stock had a massive drop and is still currently low. If there is evidence of newly appointed direction in a positive direction, this could be a high risk high reward winner. The only problem is the high risk also has the potential to become high loss and it is very hard to tell what is too late to invest.

CHAPTER 12

Retirement Planning

The "golden years" in life are considered to be the time where people have accomplished their goals and can now rest and enjoy the simpler things in life. With a little planning and the right mindset, your retirement can truly be golden. Most people falsely assume that their expenses will decrease and their tax rate will be lower. Perhaps the house will be paid off and the children will be out of college, but the increase in leisure activity has the ability to increase expenses. It's only natural for people to desire to travel and see things they haven't been able to see during their working years. It has been shown time and time again that, for most persons, spending does not decrease during retirement. This being the case, it is wiser to plan for a retirement income close to pre-retirement income. The lower tax bracket is a thing of the past. Our country is trillions of dollars in debt with Baby Boomers retiring in droves. Tax rates are more likely to increase in efforts to sustain social security and Medicare programs. With intelligent planning of assets, there is the opportunity to shelter income and reduce taxes paid. A less costly and more tax-advantaged retirement could truly be golden.

CHAPTER 13

Estate Planning

An old-fashioned term that was once quite narrow in scope is a very important issue for anyone with wealth. A common misconception is that estate planning is something that old people do just before they die. Howard explains that, in fact, planning your estate is something that is done over a lifetime, may have to be altered several times, and is critically important for people with young families. Although he does not preach, it is a sign of the responsibility of family man Howard that his goals on estate planning are quite conservative compared to his usually ambitious outlook on money management. His overall desire is the preservation and safe transfer of the assets he has built for his family.

Continuing the theme of security, Howard looks at the subject of estate planning. He gives advice on how to arrange your assets to avoid family disputes. He tells us the true story about a man who turned his will into an act of revenge against his children. A timeline is given for the preparation of a will, taking into account changes in legislation and human nature. Howard talks about various options to reduce tax liability and avoid the necessity for your family to sell assets to pay death duties. He concludes with a case study of a man who made no formal preparation and an exploration of the legality and ramifications of leaving a binding document for the distribution of assets that is not a will.

CHAPTER 14

Tax Planning

Tax planning can be an essential element to your financial independence. If you take the time to understand how tax will affect your income and use the following tax saving tips, you could keep more of your money for yourself. A good way to plan the amount of tax you will pay each year is to conduct a tax simulation to ensure you take the best strategy to minimize tax. Always remember to save a percentage of your income with interest to cover tax expenses and avoid short-term high-interest debt to pay tax.

One way to create and protect wealth is to understand and plan for taxes. Wise tax planning can help you keep more of what you earn. We all know that at least 30% of all we earn will go to taxes. This includes federal and state income taxes, social security taxes, and in some cases inheritance taxes. Higher earning individuals may pay up to 60% tax on income over a certain amount. This is why it is necessary to determine effective ways to lower tax liabilities.

CHAPTER 15

Insurance Planning

To begin analyzing your insurance needs, it is best to compare costs with several insurance companies. You can do this with the help of an insurance agent/broker or by searching and working through information from the internet. If your agent/broker is unable to provide you with a specific insurance product, you can also directly approach the company that sells the insurance. When comparing costs, be sure to consider the financial solvency and customer service ratings of the insurance company. A great way to find this information is by using rating services from companies such as A.M. Best or Standard and Poor's. These can provide you with an evaluation of an insurer or a particular insurance product. Be cautious; if a product has a too-good-to-be-true price, chances are that it is.

Insurance planning is the process of analyzing your insurance needs and finding the best method and policies that will protect your assets and family during unexpected events such as death, disability, health, and property losses. Typically, this includes an analysis of what you must protect and what risk you pass to an insurance company. This section will focus on basic information for both personal life and health insurance, as well as what you need to know when working with businesses on either group health or life insurance plans. We won't discuss property and liability insurance for businesses, as this is far more complex to cover in this section. Although insurance can provide sound financial security, you must be cautious to spend your money on the most cost-effective solutions and avoid over-insurance. Overinsurance is when you are paying more money than the potential loss that an event may incur.

CHAPTER 16

Entrepreneurship and Business Ownership

The decision to go into business for oneself, type of entrepreneurial venture, is a decision that can often require a substantial personal financial commitment. In these situations, it is often necessary to invest a great deal of one's own money to get the business off the ground. This is a high-risk, high-reward scenario, as success in this type of endeavor can lead to early retirement and a life of luxury, while a business failure can leave an entrepreneur worse off than they would have been had they stayed in the realm of being an employee.

In high school, I was confused about the topic of entrepreneurship. I thought to be an entrepreneur, you had to be in business for yourself and you had to be a business owner. I did not understand that many people can develop the traits of an entrepreneur and actually be more successful staying in the realm of being an employee. Those who fall into the category of business owners are a special breed, however. Often times, they have been risk-takers and self-starters since an early age. For these people, there is often no other road to wealth. Their commitment to success in the business world is often times fueled by the belief that they are the best person to run their business.

People generally have one of two distinct views of the rich. They either see them as a weaselly bunch who took advantage of other people to get where they are, or they think of them as self-starters who are not afraid to take risks. This is no hard and fast rule, as there are many rich people who have fallen into either category. The fact remains, however, that a higher percentage of the wealthy got there through being in business for themselves.

CHAPTER 17

Building a Strong Credit Score

The best rates on loans and most efficient credit spending will be available once a person reaches what is called an excellent credit rating. This is usually a score of 720 and up on the FICO scale of 300-850. It is important to understand that credit is a use it or lose it system and even those who have reached excellent credit can see their score go down if they shy away from credit at all.

Often, individuals who have never taken on debt or who have only used prepaid credit cards and the like have no established credit history. This will not be seen as a negative by lenders, but it will not be a positive. In these situations, it will take time to build credit and no specific borrowing and repaying is a less effective way to establish history than taking out a small loan and repaying it in a timely manner. This, of course, should not be debt that you cannot afford as taking on bad debt will be reflected on credit score for years.

A strong credit score is critical to building wealth and ensuring a secure future. Credit history determines the amount and cost of the credit available to consumers and influences the cost of insurance and auto loans. Positive credit is built by using credit responsibly over an extended period of time. This means paying bills on time, only taking on debt that you can afford, and not being overly reliant on credit.

Points based on factual information the reader of this essay might benefit from: building up a positive credit history, understanding credit scores, obtaining a free credit report, disputing mistakes, and planning for the future. Each of these will be discussed and related to the reader's overall financial plan.

CHAPTER 18

Financial Education and Literacy

Financial education is going to take a long time to produce results. However, in the long run, this should greatly help future generations to manage their finances properly.

One example of a successful project involving financial education is Boston's "Credit for Life" program, which involves high school students making mock career and lifestyle choices and spending money accordingly. This helps students to understand the impact that their choices have on their finances. A method such as this is beneficial as it is more engaging and interactive than traditional teaching and is therefore more likely to resonate with students.

Unfortunately, the United States does not place near enough emphasis on the teaching of financial education and literacy. In order to witness any sort of meaningful change in regard to the way that people manage their finances, something has to be done. This all starts with education. Measures need to be put into place to provide incentives for teachers to provide financial education to students of all ages. This will provide the young with the knowledge and skills necessary to avoid the financial pitfalls of those before them.

Financial education and literacy are seen by many as the antidote to the debt culture that currently exists in America. Whether or not you agree with that statement, what is easy to recognize is that financial education and literacy will go a long way to helping those who have been educated to properly manage their finances and to obtain and stay out of debt. There is a clear correlation between lack of financial education and debt in America.

CHAPTER 19

Mindset and Habits for Financial Success

While this still sounds oversimplified in print, behaving to attain a goal is the essence of all that has been written about changing spending habits. There is so much individual variation in how money habits are changed that it is impossible to give a complete set of instructions and there are many ways to modify the basic procedures. A good book for those interested in an in-depth self-help guide to changing behavior is "Self-Directed Behavior" by David L. Watson and Roland G. Tharp.

It is said that "virtue is its own reward." While this is a simplistic cliche, there are some virtues of wise money management which do provide direct enjoyment. Try it and see if you are not surprised at your peace of mind. A major reason for persisting in the behavior of saving is reaching the point where the saved money has begun to provide internal and external security, and freedom to do more things one wants to do. At this point it is important to avoid complacency and continuous increase in the amount and percentage of income saved.

Psychologists will tell you that all behavior is caused and maintained by its consequences. If you are to succeed in spending less and saving more you will need to increase the apparent or real pleasures of saving, or decrease the apparent or real pleasures of spending. It may seem very virtuous to say "I should not spend so much money on clothes and entertainment," but if saving is a painful duty you will likely not persist in it. Also, at the beginning of changing spending habits it will be easier to change the value you place on money and its power to bring you enjoyment, rather than working directly on behavior. The next time you go to buy something ask yourself whether the item is really worth the number of hours you had to work to buy it. You may find yourself putting the item back. Try setting a savings goal with special meaning, such as a vacation or a home, and keep a picture of the item or place near your money as a constant reminder of why you should not spend.

Once you determine the lifestyle changes you will need to make to form the habit of saving, keep in mind you are fighting a lifetime of habits formed through advertising, consumer influences, and the spending of parents. It is never easy, and never too late, to change those habits. You must want to change. If you have tried before and failed, it does not mean you are weak; only that you used the wrong approach. It is generally easier to substitute new habits for the old than to just cease the old behavior. Plan what you will do, not just what you will stop doing. A goal such as "I will save 10% of my income" is more concrete and therefore more feasible than "I will stop spending so much." If there is specific behavior you must stop, you will need to find a way to avoid situations in which you are likely to do it.

CHAPTER 20

Overcoming Financial Challenges

- Taking on a second job - Upgrading qualifications and skills, seeking promotion, looking for a better-paying job - Deferring current consumption to invest in a long-term future. For example, a person might invest in retraining to enter a new field of employment or delay childbearing to save and invest as a childfree couple for a period. - Income & benefits entitlements. Some income-poor individuals and families may be entitled to assistance or concessions that they are not receiving. This is particularly the case where the situation is temporary and the person is used to a higher standard of living. - Avoiding unemployment. The best way of dealing with low income is often to ensure that the main income earner remains employed. This may involve increasing job security through becoming an invaluable employee or by retraining and entering a career with more certain prospects.

Increasing personal/family income. No magic formula will enable low-income earners to break free from their situation, but there are a number of strategies worth considering:

The road to financial freedom is often fraught with challenges. Unexpected events such as hospitalization, the birth of a child, job loss, or divorce may often result in financial setbacks. Economic cycles and factors beyond personal control may often disrupt carefully laid plans.

Those with low income may find that no disposable income is left after essential living costs.

Overcoming financial challenges.

CHAPTER 21

Achieving Financial Independence

Formally achieving financial independence marks the end of the journey to financial freedom. This is the point where we no longer have to work for money. The money works for us. Although the road ahead is long, it is systematically planned. To maintain current lifestyle without having to work, our investments and accumulated wealth must sustain us. Obviously, if we save 10% of our income and are 50 years old, it will be another 160 years before we achieve financial freedom. If we can save a large portion of our income, say 50%, we reach our goal in 32 years. If we decrease the number of years until retirement, or increase the amount we save and invest, we obviously reach our goal sooner. Something that can drastically reduce the amount of time until we achieve financial independence is the type of investments we choose to engage in. They must generate useful income with low risk. One potential possibility might be the purchase of rental property. When our investments and accumulated wealth can provide enough income to maintain our lifestyle, it is at this point where we reach financial independence. Whether or not the goal is to reach financial independence early, the information in this book can guide you through the self-education of investing and financial management that is needed in today's uncertain economic environment.

CHAPTER 22

Generational Wealth Transfer

Effective use of different financial planning strategies will ensure clients' assets are transferred with minimal risk. The Power of Attorney (POA) can be an effective strategy in allowing a trustworthy family member to look after the financial interests of an individual who loses their mental capacity. This can lead to an Enduring Guardianship which can cover decisions on lifestyle and dignified lifestyle choices. Specific POA legislations vary from state to state, so ensure the proper instrument has been assigned to a trustworthy individual. A testamentary trust may be valid to reduce the tax impact of leaving assets directly to family members. As the most tax-effective structures are a grandchild's income has the potential to be greater than a retired person, assets may be transferred to a testamentary trust that can use income splitting provisions to maximize the after-tax benefits to the grandchild. This word use complex and should create a comfortable learning environment from the instructor to the client. Always ensure that the client has a full understanding of the use of such strategies.

"A fundamental truth in the wealth management perspective is that if financial independence has truly been achieved, then the individual will have assets that will outlast them," says Campbell. "This wealth should be transitioned in an efficient and effective manner to multiple generations. This will allow the values of the client to have a chance to be instilled into the wealth of the client's family. "How this can affect multiple generations down the family line needs to be given careful consideration," says Foster. "There may be instances where the client would want to provide education funding for a grandchild, or assistance in buying the first house for a grandchild. The relevance of providing for future generations can shape how wealth will be transferred and what sort of assets will be left behind when the client is gone."

CHAPTER 23

Philanthropy and Giving Back

At a stage just prior to retirement, defined as a point in time after which you will not accept full-time work for personal financial gain, you may choose to give a substantial amount of money as a last effort to make a difference in an issue which you have comprehended. This could be the best chance to use a lump sum amount from ending your career in investment. The impression to help others in need must not be forgotten by those entering retirement. An estate planned donation can be the final act in giving which will leave a lasting impression.

In terms of personal well-being, while you may have developed a strong satisfaction from regularly helping others, it may be possible to reach an even higher level by giving a substantial amount of your remaining working years to charity. At this time, you are still healthy and earning well with a sound comprehension of the issues faced by those in need. Time may be spent taking a more active role in helping charities.

Overall, giving can be looked at as deferred consumption. You are choosing to use your money now to assist in a problem faced by others, with the goal of reducing the problem so that there are fewer unfortunate people in the future requiring your help. Random acts of giving where one feels guilt forced to give money to someone are not recommended. An overall plan to gradually increase the proportion of both time and money used for philanthropy will result in the greatest benefits both for you as the giver and for those helped by your giving.

When it comes to donating money, many people roughly set aside a portion of their budget to be given to a charity. A more effective solution is to allocate a certain number of hours that you are paid for work and to donate all money earned in hours over that specified figure. Over time, this can become a substantial commitment. If you have surplus funds left over in your investment account after comfortably setting yourself up for the rest of your life and possibly having something for your children, you may wish to use this lump sum amount as an endowment to make a substantial difference in solving an issue faced by many.

One aspect of financial freedom and living a value-based life is giving back to those less fortunate. The best way to give can be a combination of both time and financially related acts. You should choose a charity that you are touched by and that aligns with your values, whether it is helping those less fortunate in developing countries, understanding and finding a cure for a particular sickness, or helping those locally. Spend time volunteering for the charity. This could be working at a soup kitchen, selling raffle tickets, or using your professional skills for free to help that charity. Contributing your time is often more beneficial for the charity and you than simply donating money. You get to see the direct result of your efforts at the same time as building a greater connection with your community and understanding of the issues faced by others.

CHAPTER 24

Financial Freedom and Relationships

Gaining financial freedom often precipitates a change in personal identity. This is because financial freedom involves the ability to have and do what you want without concern because of financial constraints. People will often associate their work with who they are because their job provides them with their current identity. The ability to do what you want when you want is the very essence of freedom, and therefore people sometimes find it hard to let go of their working identity. This can be further compounded if a spouse has never entered the workforce or has retired, as the working spouse may not wish to retire for concern of inconveniencing the other or losing the camaraderie they have at work.

The final set of ideas in the book considers the impact of achieving financial freedom on relationships and the broader community. This is a critical consideration for many people who want to be in a position to help themselves, then help others. The acquisition of investments can be a relatively straightforward task to complete; however, the journey towards financial freedom entails developing a new way of thinking about money and how it can be used.

CHAPTER 25

Teaching Financial Literacy

So many of the problems with finances in modern society are rooted in the fact that no one ever taught the individuals how to deal with money. School curriculum rarely covers the basics, let alone the complex issues, yet people are expected to simply know how to budget, save, invest and have a positive financial future. There are so many resources now for individuals to learn about financial literacy that was not available just a few years ago. The best place to start teaching the children of the future to be financially savvy is in their homes and in classrooms all over the world. Now that this wealth information is available, it should be included in everyday teaching by explanation and also by setting an example for the children. This type of teaching is known as incidental teaching: a parent sets an example of good spending by going to the bank, long-term saving by saving for their kids' college education, no credit debts, and so on to avoid negative consequences, by explaining reasons and lastly by getting the child involved. By setting examples and teaching informally, this is an easy and effective way of childhood teaching. Unfortunately, this was something that was ineffective for most adults since there was a lack of this information back then. So this generation and the couple after it need to learn the ins and outs of money to get on the right track. A great place for adults, teenagers, young adults to learn about money is through personal finance courses and workshops. It is never too late and this is a direct way to learn how to manage current financial situations and plan for the future. With the emphasis on money and wealth nowadays, many youth are focused on acquiring material items and an easy way to get there. Many know little of the hard work required or the types of management in between. Both the spending and saving aspects have been little touched upon and this has led to much debt and financial problems. This can be corrected if taught the basic skills of budgeting and a little bit of self-restraint. These courses are likely to be very effective given that the information is relevant and needed in today's day and age. They are also more inclined to bring a positive response given the state of the economy and how people will be forced to change their spending habits.

CHAPTER 26

Financial Freedom and Mental Health

One approach to avoiding this situation is to ensure financial security or to plan how to regain it as part of the overall recovery process from mental health problems. It may be helpful to examine the common attitudes, motivations, and values about money and to see how these, at times, may influence behavior in ways that are not conducive to financial security. Step-by-step goal setting may be a useful way of motivating and gradually moving towards financial security, and advice can be obtained from a range of information resources. The process is likely to be easier with support from a trustworthy friend, and there may be people with experience of mental health problems and money issues who can share relevant advice.

People who experience mental health problems may be particularly susceptible to financial difficulties for a number of reasons. For instance, the onset of mental health problems can lead to debts, as coping on a reduced income or having no source of income can be a huge strain. In turn, debt and financial worries can increase the amount of pressure and stress experienced, thus worsening the mental health problem.

Put bluntly, poverty is a cause of mental health problems, and mental health problems are a cause of poverty. Poverty can seriously affect your mental health. Not having enough material resources can be a major source of stress, anxiety, and depression. Having a mental health problem makes you more vulnerable to ending up in poverty. Not only do many people have extra costs – for example, for medications or higher fuel bills – but they are also less able to earn money because of discrimination and the disabling effects of their condition.

CHAPTER 27

Financial Freedom at Different Life Stages

Life stage is a determinant of income, expenses, assets, debts, and responsibilities. This, in turn, influences the capacity to save, invest, and insure and affects the time taken to achieve financial freedom. Heather provides case studies of two families at different life stages. The analysis identifies their strategies for improving their financial situation and the reasons for these strategies. This shows why different approaches may be wise for different people and that there is not a 'one size fits all' solution. An understanding of the strategy best suited to their own situation is the key message that Heather wishes to give readers as they approach different life stages on their journey to financial freedom.

In this section, Heather sets out specific strategies for achieving financial freedom at different life stages, from young adulthood to retirement. She encourages the reader to take a systematic approach, including assessing their current financial position, setting goals and targets, and considering the risks along the way. By paying off debts and accumulating income-generating assets, many people will achieve financial freedom before retirement age. For those who are unable to follow these guidelines and for women who may not have been involved in financial decision making, managing superannuation to provide a good income in retirement is a key issue.

Financial freedom at different life stages

CHAPTER 28

Financial Freedom and Work-Life Balance

Imagine that we split a $10,000,000 inheritance between you and a friend. You are given your $5,000,000 share entirely in cash. After carefully paying off all debts, you are left with $4,000,000 and you decide to invest it to ensure a future lifestyle and to leave something for loved ones or charitable causes. This investment can be easily and safely placed in low-risk accounts that pay annual interest and/or dividends of 4%, adjusting for inflation. This means you can spend $160,000 per year and expect that your post-inflation standard of living will be maintained. Now the closer the $160,000 is to your current standard of living, the closer you are to achieving financial freedom.

Most people want to achieve financial freedom because it will enable them to be free to do other things that they value with their lives. The concept of financial freedom has been used in many different ways with a multitude of meanings, but it is generally used to describe the state of having sufficient personal wealth to live without having to work actively for basic necessities. For financially free people, their assets generate income that is greater than their expenses. If you have achieved financial freedom, work becomes a matter of choice instead of necessity, ensuring more time is available for you to do things you prefer to do. Take the following quiz to determine how close you are to achieving financial freedom.

CHAPTER 29

Financial Freedom and Personal Development

Personal development must occur before you can experience financial freedom. A lesson often learned the hard way, many individuals tirelessly strive to achieve financial independence in an effort to create a better life for themselves or their families. However, the passion driven towards accomplishing this goal often obscures the true meaning of success, causing many to miss the vital lessons learned along the way. In the end, all the money in the world cannot bring about true happiness if it has been gained at the expense of integrity, health, or family. If you sacrifice your wellbeing or your family to expand your financial empire, you will have defeated the purpose of achieving any success. Therefore, it is important that you expand yourself, mentally, physically, emotional and spiritually in order to handle the responsibilities that come with increased financial wealth. By doing this you will increase the quality of your life and the lives of those around you. Financial freedom is the absence of worry in an individual due to having achieved a balance between what they earn and what they spend. It is not about becoming rich. It is a state of well-being where a person is able to fully experience life knowing that they have the financial means to support the lifestyle they desire. People should understand how to utilize this financial freedom to better themselves and the society around them.

CHAPTER 30

Financial Freedom and Travel

At one time, we could only afford long weekend trips. For a few precious vacation days, we would suffer a 5-hour drive with 4 adults and one child in a small sedan to the Northern California coast to pitch a tent in a friend's wet and cold backyard. Later, we enjoyed a weekend jaunt to the same area staying in a motel and dining out. Our quality of travel improved significantly when our income reached six figures. We ventured to Europe twice and enjoyed Mexico on three occasions. But even at those income levels, those trips seemed far too short. It was often difficult to communicate with newfound friends and acquaintances due to language barriers, and our attempts at practicing foreign language skills were awkward. We longed for a better way to immerse ourselves in the cultures of other lands.

We have always enjoyed traveling. Over the years, we have taken many vacations both within the United States and abroad. Our experiences before and after achieving financial freedom help us to explain the advantages in the quality of those experiences and the benefits to enjoyment at both ends of the financial flexibility spectrum.

CHAPTER 31

Financial Freedom and Health

To address this issue, focus on improving your health. We are all aware that our health is our ultimate wealth. This is true because without good health, there is no energy to pursue financial ambitions or enjoy the fruits of your labor. The powerful link between health and wealth means that it is essential to keep in good health during your journey to financial freedom. Medical problems can have a devastating effect on your finances and push you backwards on your path to financial security. Approximately 50% of personal bankruptcies result from unpaid medical expenses and 100% of bankruptcies resulting from medical expenses are filed by people who have health insurance. This is because protection provided by health insurance is often inadequate. It is generally much easier to obtain finance for healthcare than it is to save money to invest for future healthcare needs. Step one of the plan to safeguard your finances from potential devastation as a result of poor health is to lead a healthy lifestyle. This is often easier to do when compared to the potential alternatives of working longer to repay debts or regaining lost savings. Step two is to obtain adequate protection to isolate health incidents from your finances. This is often in the form of health insurance, income protection, and trauma/critical illness insurance. Document your plan in your financial strategy to ensure that these methods are not viewed as an expense on your finances, but instead as a method to achieve the ultimate cost-effective result. This is to be in good health without the financial burden of health incidents. A common mistake made by people is to neglect their current dental and health needs through lack of insurance coverage due to the confidence that they are young and healthy. The consequences of unexpected health incidents can be financially devastating, and it is impossible to ensure when good health will no longer be something that can be taken for granted. Always be prepared for the unexpected.

Conclusion

The road to financial freedom starts at the corner of hard work and perseverance, breaking through your personal wall of self-doubt and taking the initiative to change the way we perceive the concept of money. From high school students, college students, or even middle-aged people with families, we should all take action now. Seemingly impossible, minor adjustments in your life will create a change in your future. Get rid of those high-interest credit cards and get something that takes money out of your bank account. Set up a monthly due date spreadsheet to remind yourself when your bills are due, and then start direct depositing your checks to skip one more step in getting paid. Give yourself a limit on certain expenses, and track those expenses throughout the month using an expense journal. All of these things require a little more effort than what you are used to but are only more efficient ways of managing the money you work so hard to attain. An example of this would be Mrs. Sally Smith. On the outside, she is a mild-mannered nurse, but in personal she is a dedicated cookie lover. revealed that her favorite cookies are Anise flavored and that she would travel to Mexico to find them. After tracking her expenses in an expense journal, she comes to the realization of spending close to $400 a month on these cookies, saying "I had no idea, it never seemed like I was spending that much on something so little". Upon discovering this, Mrs. Sally Smith succeeded in limiting herself to only $50 a month on her special cookie. Although this is only an example, tiny discoveries such as these are the cornerstones of effective money management.